MONUMENTAL MILESTONES
GREAT EVENTS OF MODERN TIMES

Exploring the North Pole:
The Story of Robert Edwin
Peary and Matthew Henson

Robert Peary photographed Matthew
Henson, center, and their four Inuit
guides on April 8, 1909, at the North Pole.

Mitchell Lane
PUBLISHERS

P.O. Box 196
Hockessin, Delaware 19707
www.mitchelllane.com

Titles in the Series

The Dawn of Aviation:
The Story of the Wright Brothers

The Story of the Attack on Pearl Harbor

Breaking the Sound Barrier:
The Story of Chuck Yeager

Top Secret: The Story of the
Manhattan Project

The Story of the Holocaust

The Civil Rights Movement

Exploring the North Pole:
The Story of Robert Edwin
Peary and Matthew Henson

The Story of the Great Depression

The Cuban Missile Crisis:
The Cold War Goes Hot

The Fall of the Berlin Wall

Disaster in the Indian Ocean,
Tsunami 2004

MONUMENTAL MILESTONES
GREAT EVENTS OF MODERN TIMES

Exploring the North Pole: The Story of Robert Edwin Peary and Matthew Henson

Robert Peary photographed Matthew Henson, center, and their four Inuit guides on April 8, 1909, at the North Pole.

Josepha Sherman

Printing   1   2   3   4   5   6   7   8   9

Library of Congress Cataloging-in-Publication Data
Sherman, Josepha
    Exploring the North Pole: the story of Robert Edwin Peary and Matthew Henson/
By Josepha Sherman.
        p. cm.—(Monumental Milestones)
    Includeds bibliographical references and index.
    ISBN 1-58415-402-0
1. Peary, Robert E. (Robert Edwin), 1856-1920—Juvenile literature. 2. Henson, Matthew Alexander, 1866-1955—Juvenile literature. 3. Explorers—United States—Biography—Juvenile literature. 4. African American explorers—Biography—Juvenile literature. 5. North Pole—Discovery and exploration—Juvenile literature. I. Title. II. Series.
    G634.S54 2005
    910'.9163'2—dc22

                                                                            2005004246

ABOUT THE AUTHOR: Josepha Sherman is a prolific author with more than 60 books in print. The owner of Sherman Editorial Services, Josepha has also written a six-book series on alternative energy (Capstone); *The History of the Internet* (Franklin Watts); *Bill Gates: Computer King* (Millbrook); and *Henry Cavendish and the Discovery of Hydrogen* and *J. J. Thomson and the Discovery of Electrons* (both for Mitchell Lane Publishers). In addition, this native New Yorker has a degree in archaeology, loves to tinker with computers, and follows the NY Mets.

PHOTO CREDITS: Cover, pp. 1, 3 Library of Congress; p. 6 Jamie Kondrchek; pp. 10, 16 Library of Congress, p. 26 Andrea Pickens; p. 28 Library of Congress; p. 25 National Archives at College Park, Maryland; pp. 28, 36 Library of Congress

PUBLISHER'S NOTE: This story is based on the author's research, which she believes to be accurate. Documentation of such research is on page 46.
The internet sites referenced herein were active as of the publication date. Due to the fleeting nature of some websites, we cannot guarantee they will all be active when you are reading this book.

Contents

Exploring the North Pole: The Story of Robert Edwin Peary and Matthew Henson

Josepha Sherman

The cold continent of Greenland lies less than 500 miles from the North Pole.

At about three times the size of Texas, Greenland is the world's largest island. Over 80 percent of the country—all but a thin strip of land around the coast—is covered in ice.

On the Edge of the World

They were two men alone in the middle of nowhere. American explorer Robert Peary and Danish explorer Christian Maigaard were stranded in the frozen wastes of Greenland, miles from the rest of their party's base camp. They had gone off to explore together. Without realizing it, they had trekked too far into the icy wilderness. Now they had only a few days of food left. If the men didn't quickly find a way back to the camp, they would starve or freeze to death.

Peary had an idea. It would be a wild gamble, and if it failed, they would both die. But there was no other solution that either man could find. And if they didn't try this, they would definitely die.

Peary threw all the supplies off their two sleds and tied the sleds together. He made a sail out of their bedding, and a rudder out of an ax. They had an iceboat! Peary and Maigaard flew along the ice for hours. They began to hope that their plan would work. It had to work! They had no food left at all now, and no spare clothing.

Suddenly great crevasses, giant cracks in the ice, gaped before them. The men were going so fast, they wouldn't be able to stop in time!

They didn't try to slow down. Their iceboat flew over the crevasses and slammed down on the other side. The wind caught their sail again with such force that they went flying on down the ice at breakneck speed. They were going to make it!

Then they approached a larger crevasse. It was too wide for them to sail across. They managed to stop—on the very edge. There was only one narrow bridge of ice over that deep gash. Peary and Maigaard eased their way along it. When the sleds were halfway across, the ice bridge collapsed! Peary was already on solid ice, but Maigaard was not. He was hanging on to the sleds, and the sleds were sliding into the crevasse.

As Peary later wrote: "For a moment [the sleds] hung tilted over the chasm, with a man's life hanging on [them]." Peary threw his weight forward onto his end of the sleds, balancing them. Maigaard, shaken but unhurt, was able to pull himself onto solid ice.[1]

They'd made it. At base camp, the rest of their party was waiting for them.

Even though they had nearly died, Peary wasn't going to give up. This time he hadn't gotten too far. He would try again. And when he did, he vowed, he was going to explore much farther north.

He would reach the North Pole.

FOR YOUR INFORMATION

The North and South Poles

The North and South Poles are often depicted as two tall columns or even barber poles sticking out of the ground. But the poles don't actually exist. They are two points on Earth's axis. The axis is a line through the center of Earth about which the planet turns. The North Pole is the "top" of the axis, about four hundred miles from any solid ground, and the South Pole is the "bottom," in the middle of Antarctica. On a map, the North Pole lies at latitude 90° North. The South Pole lies at 90° South. (The equator is at 0° latitude.)

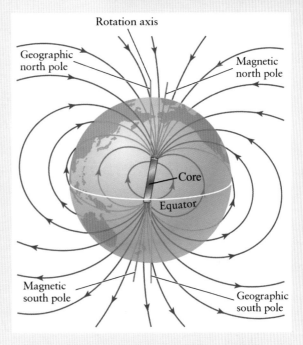

The North Pole has always seemed mysterious. It is so remote and cold that for ages no one knew what was up there. The mystery brought scores of curious explorers, many of whom failed to reach

Earth's magnetic field (blue lines) give the planet north and south magnetic poles. These poles differ from Earth's north and south geographic poles.

their destination. By the 21st century, thousands of people had visited the North Pole. In fact, every year a challenging event is held there: the North Pole Marathon. That's right. People run a race that circles the North Pole. In one race, they run all the way around the world—several times.

There are two other poles that aren't the same as the geographic North and South Poles. These are the north and south magnetic poles. Earth's core is magnetized; it makes it seem as if there's a giant bar magnet running through the planet. A magnet has a positive end, or pole, and a negative pole. The positive pole pulls things to it, while the negative pole pushes things away. When a person uses a compass, Earth's magnetism causes the needle to point north.

The magnetic poles are not fixed in one place the way the geographic North and South Poles are. They have moved back and forth over centuries. Earth's magnetic field has even reversed its polarity several times. When the polarity reverses, the positive "top" of the planet and the negative "bottom" of the planet swap powers. Will this happen in the future? Probably. When it does, though, scientists agree that life will go right on for everyone.

9

Robert Peary wears traditional Inu
made from the fur of Arctic anima

When Peary thought of
going to the North Pole,
he wondered why no one
had thought to ask for
help from the Inuit.

Beginnings

Robert Edwin Peary was born in the small town of Cresson, Pennsylvania, on May 6, 1856 (some accounts claim that he was born in the nearby town of Chester Springs). No one expected the boy to be anything special. After all, there was nobody at all famous or unusual on either side of his family going back several generations.

But then something unusual and tragic did happen to the Peary family. Robert's father, Charles Peary, died suddenly at age 30, when his son was only three. Robert's mother, Mary, had never really recovered from the baby's birth. Though sickly, she was gentle and kind. She could, however, also be quite strong-willed. When her husband died so suddenly, Mary flatly refused to ever marry again. She also flatly refused to stay in Pennsylvania a moment longer than was necessary to take care of her husband's funeral. She returned to her native Maine, taking her baby with her.

Right from the start, Mary Peary had problems with her son. Robert wasn't a bad boy, and he and his mother loved each other, but he was a very active child. He was curious about everything, and he liked to play tricks on people. Because of this, he was always getting into trouble. It didn't help that his mother soon showed that she had no idea how to raise a conventional boy. She tried to raise him as a girl, teaching him how to sew and knit, and attempted to keep him nice and gentle. She was always worrying about his health, even though Robert almost never got sick. Robert had very fair skin and got sunburned easily. His mother made him wear a girl's sunbonnet to protect him. Not surprisingly, Robert got into a lot of fights in his early days.

At last Mary Peary gave up trying to turn her son into something he wasn't. When Robert was 12, she sent him away to boarding school. That was the best thing she could have done for both Robert and herself. Robert missed his mother at first, but soon was sending her letters that said things like, "I have had a pretty good time since you left me."[1]

Robert was always very interested in natural history. He even spent some of his precious money—40 cents, which was a lot of money in the 19th century—to hear a series of lectures on geology, the study of the earth. Throughout his teenage years, Robert went on as many nature trips and hunting trips as he could manage, and he enjoyed them very much.

In 1873, Robert graduated. He decided to go on to Bowdoin College in Brunswick, Maine, where he planned to study civil engineering, the science of building things. There was no money to send him to college, but he earned a full scholarship. By this time, Robert adored anything to do with the outdoors. Taxidermy, the art of preserving and stuffing dead animals to make them look alive, was very popular at the time. Robert became skilled in mounting dead hawks and eagles, studying them as he worked. He did well in college, graduating in second place of all the graduates, and earning a degree in civil engineering, as he'd planned. But once he had the degree, what was he to do with himself?

Robert and his mother stayed in Maine. For a time, he made a living in the small towns of the area as a surveyor. He dated some of the local girls, but nothing came of that. All the time that he was in rural Maine, Robert was growing more and more restless. He wrote to his mother on August 16, 1880: "Here I am, twenty-four years old, and what have I done? What am I doing, or what am I in the way of doing? Nothing."[2]

The following year, Robert made the break with small-town life. He passed an exam that made him a civil engineer for the U.S. Navy. On October 26, 1881, he was named a lieutenant of the Civil Engineer Corps. He was sent to Florida to oversee the construction of a dock for the navy. The men there were used to working in the cooler north. They had no idea how to build something in Florida's tropical heat. It took courage for a young lieutenant to cancel a navy order, but he did it.

During that mission, Peary got the idea of becoming an explorer. He happily accepted a new mission to Nicaragua, in Central America. He was to survey the country for a possible canal that could connect the Atlantic and Pacific Oceans. In a letter to his mother dated December 20, 1884, Robert called the country "the land which first gladdened the eyes of Columbus." This might have been when Peary first thought about trekking to the North Pole, because he added, "Columbus . . . whose fame can be equalled only by . . . the discoverer of the North Pole."[3]

In July 1885, Peary, still in Nicaragua, was browsing in a used bookstore when he found a pamphlet titled, *Conjectures on the Inland Ice of Greenland.* Why did he buy it? No one knows, but that pamphlet triggered something in Peary. When he was a boy, he had been fascinated with the Arctic, the far north. The pamphlet may have stirred up that old fascination. For the next year, Peary read everything he could find on the subject. He knew that there had been earlier attempts to reach the North Pole. He knew that they had all failed. And two questions remained unanswered. Why had none of the earlier expeditions sought the help of the northern people, the Inuit? (Peary knew them as Eskimos, the old name for the Inuit.) And why had the explorers all tried to sail to the North Pole rather than traveling north over the solid ice of Greenland?

In the late 19th century, there were no airplanes. No one knew what lay to the far north. There was no way of knowing that Greenland was actually an island. It did seem possible in those days that Greenland might stretch all the way to the North Pole.

By 1886, Peary was determined to go. His mother, even though she thought that this idea of her son's was a wild one, lent him the money. Then Peary was invited to speak in front of the National Academy of Sciences in Washington. This was his chance, he thought. He told them, "I propose making a trip to Greenland this summer [to obtain] scientific information . . . and at the same time to test my ideas in regards to methods and equipment."[4]

Peary did not get any help from the academy, but at least they listened to him. The navy listened to him, too. They didn't think Peary would succeed, but they must have believed something about his request, because they gave him six months' leave.

Peary was ready for his first Arctic exploration.

Henry Hudson

The Europeans' hunt for the North Pole and a water route to Asia—the Northern Passage—began in 1587, when English explorer John Davis sailed up the coast of Greenland for about eight hundred miles. At the time, it was the farthest north anyone had ever sailed. Over the next 20 years, many other explorers tried to find the Northern Passage, but no one did. Their wooden ships weren't designed to withstand the cold and ice.

In 1607, English explorer Henry Hudson, sailing for the Dutch, did explore a great deal of the North Atlantic. On a later mission to the North Atlantic, in 1611, he died on the ice. Over the next two centuries, Dutch ships followed his path, not to find the North Pole but to take advantage of the good fishing that Hudson had reported.

The next attempt was made in 1819 by English explorer Sir William Parry, who made it halfway from Greenland to the Bering Strait. The attempt failed when Parry was defeated by open stretches of water and currents that carried him back every time he tried to go forward. His attempt was followed in 1829 by English explorer John Ross, who tried steam power. His steamboat's engine wasn't strong enough to withstand the stress put on it by the cold and ice. However, Ross did discover the precise location of the magnetic north pole.

Next came the major expedition of Sir John Franklin in 1845. Franklin set out with two ships, the *Erebus* and the *Terror*. His party was well equipped. Franklin seemed able, if anyone was, to reach the North Pole. But tragedy struck when the ships became trapped in the ice. The party was forced to abandon their ships and strike out on foot. None survived. An Inuit woman reported that the starving, exhausted men "fell down and died as they walked."[5]

One of those sent out to try to rescue the Franklin party was American Elisha Kent Kane, captaining the *Advance*. He failed to find the Franklin ships, but he did explore what is now called Kane Basin, a passage to the polar sea.

The next major mission came in 1871, when American Charles Hall set sail for the north aboard the *Polaris*. That mission, too, was stopped short by the ice. Hall died of a heart attack, but many of his crew survived by taking refuge on an ice floe and riding it out into open water, where they were rescued by another ship.

This mission was followed by many other American and British sea attempts—and all of them were defeated by the ice and terrible cold. Everyone knew that the North Pole was there, but no one seemed able to reach it.

Matthew Henson wears a white fox fur hood made by Inuit women.

Henson got along well with the Inuit people. He learned their language and their survival skills, and they trusted him. They called him "Miy Paluk," meaning "Matthew the Kind One."

The Early Trips

Getting to Greenland wasn't a problem for Peary. He quickly found passage aboard the whaling ship *Eagle.* Deciding what gear to take was another matter. Peary knew he needed a lightweight sled, light enough for him to pull but sturdy enough to hold together no matter how rough the land. It had to be large enough to hold food, water, and clothing, plus snowshoes and skis.

Reaching Greenland in 1887, he met up with Danish explorer Christian Maigaard. They made it about a hundred miles north, but that was as far as they could get. Their adventures together ended with that wild trip down the ice on their sled-boat.

Peary couldn't be too disappointed with having to return to life in the United States and Nicaragua. He met a young woman named Josephine—Jo—Diebitsch, and by midsummer, they were engaged to be married. Photographs of Jo show a lovely young woman with lively eyes. Neither Robert nor Jo wanted to wait for a formal wedding. They were married in August 1888. It appears to have been a happy marriage. Robert even dedicated one of his books to her, *Nearest the Pole,* in which he says, "To her who has been my constant aid and inspiration and who has borne the brunt of it all."[1]

For several years, the brunt that Jo bore was Robert's frustration. He was torn between carrying out his navy duty in Nicaragua and wanting to return to Greenland. He wanted to be the first to cross it. Only six months after his marriage, Peary learned that a Norwegian explorer, Fridtjof Nansen, had done it. Nansen had only crossed from east to west at the narrow southern tip of the island—but it had been a crossing. Peary was stunned but more determined than ever to return to the Arctic. He began a letter-writing campaign to everyone he thought might help him, including Nansen. Peary wrote about geography, stating how little was actually known about Greenland. He wrote about anthropology, the scientific study of people, stating how little was known about the Inuit way of life. He lectured about anything to do with Arctic exploration.

Meanwhile, Peary needed an assistant in Nicaragua. He picked a young man he'd met in Washington, D.C., Matthew A. Henson, or Matt, as he preferred to be called.

In the 21st century, at least in the United States, many people have begun to take civil rights for granted. Discrimination against anyone because of race, color, or religion is illegal. But at the end of the 19th century, few African Americans were allowed to hold any important jobs. Matt, who had been born in Maryland on August 8, 1866, the year after the Civil War and slavery ended, was the son of free black parents. They died when he was still a child. At age 12, Matt walked the approximately 37 miles from Washington, D.C., to Baltimore, Maryland, where he got a job as a cabin boy aboard a merchant ship called the

Katie Hines. Its captain, Captain Childs, took in the orphaned boy and taught him all about the sea. He also tutored him in math, history, geography, and even carpentry.

When Matt was nearly 20, Captain Childs died. Matt lost all interest in the sea, but then found what he hadn't really realized while with the kindly captain—there were few good jobs for a young African-American man. He finally found a job as a clerk in a clothing and hat store in Washington, D.C. It was a far cry from his dawning dreams of adventure.

At the clerk job, he met Robert Peary, who was looking for a hat to take to Nicaragua. Peary didn't care about Henson's race. The two talked for some time, and they liked each other. Henson shared Peary's love of exploration. He happily left his predictable job to go with Peary to Nicaragua as his assistant. It was a good choice for both of them. Peary soon found that Henson was sharp-witted and had very useful skills as a mechanic, navigator, and carpenter. He put Henson in charge of the entire camp of 145 people.

After Nicaragua, Peary helped Henson get a job at the League Island Navy Yard in Philadelphia. Both men knew that it was just a temporary thing, and that Peary planned to take Henson with him on any future Arctic expeditions. Henson was delighted with that prospect. His fiancée, Eva Flint, was not so happy about it. Perhaps she thought that there never would be another expedition, or that Matt would never leave her to go on one, because she and Henson were married in April 1891.

Two months later, all of Peary's hard work paid off. Three scientific organizations teamed up to sponsor him. They were the American Geographical Society, the Brooklyn Institute, and the Philadelphia Academy of Natural Sciences. The navy agreed to give him another leave of absence. His North Greenland Expedition set sail from New York on a ship named the *Kite* on June 6, 1891. It was a party of seven, including Henson—and, to many people's surprise, Jo. She was the first white woman ever to travel so far north. The Inuit people were amazed to see her.

Many people were also surprised that Peary had chosen Henson to join his expedition. They often referred to Henson only as a servant rather than as a true assistant. They even asked why Peary hadn't taken a white man instead of a black man. For Peary, Henson's color didn't matter, only that he was intelligent and adventurous.

On July 11, their journey was almost ended before it had truly gotten going. Peary broke his leg. Although the doctors on board the *Kite* set the leg skillfully, Peary was forced to oversee the setting up of a winter base without being able to stand. In fact, he was off his feet for many weeks.

When Robert and Jo found out that August 8 was Henson's birthday, there in the Arctic, they threw him his first ever real birthday party. Jo cooked a huge feast. Henson was very touched.

While Peary recovered, he and Henson got to know the Inuit. Henson was quick to pick up the Inuit language and to understand their ways. He was honored to be charged with the care of an orphaned Inuit boy, Kudlooktoo. Peary had been told that the Inuit were a lazy, dirty people, but he knew, both from what Henson told him and from his own observations, that that description wasn't true. Peary had also reasoned that anyone who had managed to live in the Arctic for so many centuries certainly had some knowledge worth learning. The Inuit saved their energy. When there was nothing to be done, they played indoor games or rested, just like anyone else. But when there was hunting to be done, they were all business. They were dirty only by American standards, and only because there was no easy way to bathe in the frozen Arctic. Peary also found them, in general, to be loving and utterly honest. Jo gave them cloth and steel needles, which the women were glad to have; they had been using bone needles, which worked with heavy materials like fur and leather but couldn't sew fine stitches. Above all, the Inuit prized anything of wood. There was almost no wood in the Arctic other than bits of driftwood that would wash up on the shores of Greenland. They fueled their fires with whale blubber.

Peary and Henson knew that befriending the Inuit would prove to be invaluable. Peary wrote, "With their help, the world shall discover the North Pole."[2]

For the winter camp, Peary took a lesson from the Inuit, saying that if they could live comfortably through the winter, so could he. Using Henson's carpentry skills, the men built a winter house in Inuit style, with an outer wall and an inner wall and four rooms. The outer wall was built out of the barrels of supplies that would be preserved by the freezing weather. The air between the two walls acted as insulation to help protect the men from the cold. A stove was dug into the earth floor like a fire pit so that it would heat the air and yet not pose a great risk of accidental fires. Heavy blankets of cheerful red were hung on the inner walls both to cut down on the drafts and to add some color to the house. The men slept on cots, wrapped in furs.[3]

Danger, however, was always waiting. Once one of the men accidentally knocked down a box of matches. The whole box caught fire, as Peary puts it, "in all directions." He describes the wild comedy that followed. "Dr. [Frederick] Cook . . . sprang out [of his bunk] in his sleeping bag and fell, half-awake, on the matches on all fours, just in time to encounter, full in the face, a pailful of water which I had thrown." By the time the fire was out, Dr. Cook had been drenched by three pails of water.[4]

Another incident was more serious. Once Peary could walk again, he and two other men, Eivind Astrup and Dr. Cook, set out to explore a little. They hadn't yet learned how to read the weather. Caught in a terrible storm, they took shelter in a snow house they'd had to build. It wasn't as well made as an Inuit igloo. That night, the storm's fierce winds tore a hole in the shelter. The house was instantly filled with snow, and the party was nearly buried alive. They managed to struggle outside—but they were in their sleeping bags and without their outer clothing. Peary knew that if they huddled together, they would stay warm for a day or so. But if the storm didn't die down, they would be unable to dig down through the snow for their outer clothing and their food. They would be doomed. At last the storm did end, and they were able to recover both their food and their warm clothing.

In addition to the other hardships, there was the long darkness of winter, during which Peary and his party could do little but wait. In the far north, there are summer days when the sun shines for nearly 24 hours. But in the winter, there are months during which the sun never rises at all. Peary wrote, "It may well be doubted if . . . a person who has never experienced four months

of constant darkness [can] imagine what it is. . . . Only he who has risen and gone to bed by lamplight . . . day after day, week after week, month after month, can know how beautiful is the sunlight."[5]

Henson adds a description of the long, seemingly endless winter night: "Not a sound, except the report of a glacier, broken off by its weight, and causing a new iceberg to be born." He continues, "The black darkness of the sky, the stars twinkling above, and hour after hour going by with no sunlight . . . and always the cold . . . ."[6]

By May 1892, the long winter was over. On May 3, Peary set out on his journey of exploration, heading north across the ice. He took three men with him, Cook, Astrup, and Langdon Gibson, the team's ornithologist, or bird expert. Each man had a sled, and they shared a pack of 20 sled dogs. On the sleds were food, snowshoes, skis, and scientific instruments for recording temperature and location.

By May 24, Cook and Gibson turned back. Peary went on with Astrup and 14 dogs. The trip was a nightmare. There were long stretches of snow too soft to support the sleds. The men had to help the dogs drag them. Many of the dogs died. There were almost constant and unpredictable storms. Dazzling sunlight alternated with thick fog. But they crossed the ice and at last reached Greenland's rocky northern shore. Peary described the scene: "Before us stretched new lands and waters. . . . It was almost impossible . . . to believe that we were standing upon the northern shore of Greenland . . . with the most brilliant sunlight . . . with yellow poppies growing between the rocks."[7]

The men planted an American flag there. Then came the long and just as terrible trip back to the base camp. They made it without a loss. However, when they returned, they found that one of the other men had gone off on an exploration of his own from the base camp. He had died. Saddened by the loss, Peary and his party boarded the *Kite* and sailed for home.

Once Peary had achieved his goal of crossing Greenland, he was happy—but only for a short while. There was so much that was still to be discovered. He wanted to see it all. The Arctic was such a fascinating place, he thought. Even though he had nearly been killed on this expedition, he could hardly wait for another expedition to begin.

Starting another expedition wasn't going to be as easy as he had thought. His successful journey had captured the imagination of the public. They hailed him as a hero. But the navy, although proud of him, didn't want to let him go off again. They wanted him to stay and work for the navy. It took a great deal of negotiating to win Peary more time off. He hated public speaking, but he and Henson raised money for another expedition by giving lively lectures about their adventures. After Peary spoke, Henson, dressed in his furs and cracking a whip, would drive a dogsled team across the stage.

All that work did the trick. In June 1893, Peary and Henson set sail for Greenland aboard a ship called the *Falcon*. With them once again was Peary's wife. She was expecting their first child in September. People thought that Robert and Jo were crazy to take such a chance, but neither of them was worried about it. Jo was in perfect health, and they had a good doctor in their party.

On September 12, Jo gave birth in Greenland to a little girl. The Inuit men and women had never seen such a white baby. Even though they knew she was real and not made out of snow, they gave the little girl the nickname of Ahnighito, or Snowbaby. Robert and Jo named her Marie, but the nickname stuck.

Their daughter's birth was about the only thing to go right with the expedition. The weather was against them. Many of their supplies of food and fuel were lost in an avalanche. Harsh winds blew for days without stopping. Storms rose up without warning. By 1894, Robert had to give up. His expedition this time had been a failure.

However, he wasn't giving up on the idea of making other explorations. When the *Falcon* arrived ahead of schedule, Robert put Jo and Marie on board. Many of the men in his party left, too. In fact, only two men decided to stay with Robert: his assistants Hugh Lee and Matt Henson.

The three men set out for the other side of Greenland. They nearly died. Lee fell ill, and so did some of their dogs. The supplies ran out. Henson managed to shoot a hare, but that wasn't very much food for even one man. Then, just when they were on the verge of starvation, they reached the coast and managed to kill some musk oxen. The men and the dogs ate and ate.

On the trip back, they were out of food again, and lost all but one dog. If anything had happened to the base camp, Peary, Henson, and Lee would die.

But the home camp was fine. For a month after reaching it, the three men did nothing but rest and eat, eat and rest. In 1895, the ship returned, and they gladly set sail for home.

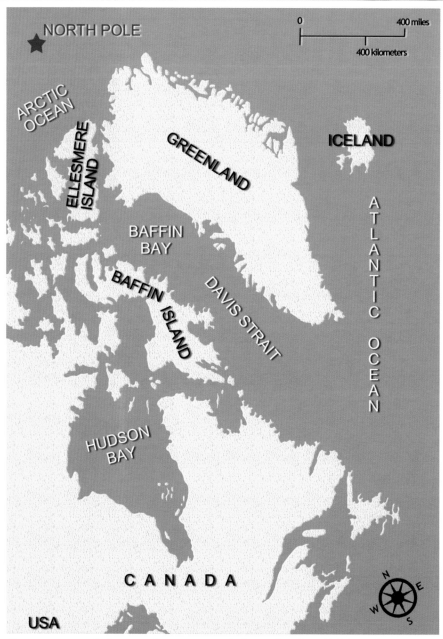

Peary crossed the northern part of Greenland in 1892 with Astrup and in 1895 with Henson and Lee. An icy sea separates Greenland from the North Pole. The ice around the pole changes shape and size as the water freezes and melts throughout the year.

The Arctic may seem like a place where no one would or could live. There are long months of bitter cold, and months of almost total darkness. But people are determined. The various different tribal groups who live in the Arctic region around the world have been there for thousands of years. They aren't all related. They range from the Inuit tribes of Alaska and Canada to the Saami of northern Finland and the Chukchi of Siberia. They have all devised ways of dealing with their harsh surroundings. The Saami and Chukchi, for instance, are reindeer herders. The other groups hunt fish and northern animals such as reindeer (also called caribou), walrus, and seals.

A young Inuit

Peary and Henson knew the most about the Inuit of Greenland. Although today many Inuit live in modern towns, in the 1890s, the Inuit were hunters who lived off fish, seal, and walrus. They followed the game inland or down the coast, depending on the season. They used tools and harpoons made out of bone or stone—though by Peary and Henson's time, traders had also given the Inuit some metal tools, too.

The Inuit also used the animals they caught for things other than food, such as for lamp oil and clothing. Although the Inuit are associated with living in igloos, huts made of blocks of ice, they used these only for short stays. For permanent structures, they dug out homes from the earth and covered them with driftwood roofs. Using bone needles, the Inuit women sewed clothing out of hide and fur. The Inuit also invented the kayak, a type of skin-covered canoe that is easy to maneuver and almost impossible to keep tipped over.

The Inuit in the 1890s had deliberately never been as far north as the North Pole. In their belief, the area was an evil place, ruled over by Kokoyah, the God of the Ice Cap. It was a place that was too dangerous for mere humans to visit.

Today, anthropologists—scientists who study human beings and their culture—suspect that, unlike what Peary and those of his time thought, the different peoples of the North had been in contact with one another ever since the Inuit first traveled across North America thousands of years ago.

Josephine Peary kept a journal of adventures.

She traveled with Robert on two Greenland expeditions, and gave birth to daughter Marie in Greenland.

The Pole

By the end of the 1890s, Peary was ready to try again. With the help of government officials—and possibly with the agreement of President William McKinley—he was granted five years' leave from the navy for Arctic exploration. Henson would have to leave his job at New York's American Museum of Natural History, where for two years he had worked on exhibits of Arctic life.

In 1897, Peary and Henson made their attempt, reaching the site of a tragic failed expedition. This one had been made in 1881 by U.S. Army Lieutenant A. W. Greeley. He and his men had starved to death. Peary couldn't help feeling a little contemptuous over the needless deaths. If Greeley and his men had studied the land before setting out, and had talked with the Inuit, they would have realized that there was good hunting in the area.

This trip soon turned into a personal disaster for Peary. In the middle of the dark, freezing northern winter, he noticed "a suspicious wooden feeling" in his feet. Peary's feet were seriously frostbitten. Henson tried to thaw them by holding them under his shirt, and he managed to keep an infection from spreading, but in the end eight of Peary's toes had to be amputated. He was temporarily helpless, flat on his back in camp for six weeks.

At first he was in despair. Had all of the frostbitten area been removed? Would he lose more of his feet, or even his legs?

Luckily the frostbite had not spread. Peary was determined to recover. He writes, "I never lost faith, in spite of the . . . statements of my physician that [I] could never again walk effectively. I knew that I should yet do the work which I had set before myself."[1] And Peary did, indeed, walk again.

The trip was a personal disaster for Henson as well. Eva, tired of always having to worry about her husband and never having him with her, divorced him in 1897. They had been married for six years, but she had seen him during that time for less than two years.

News was slow in reaching Peary in his Arctic camp. In 1899, he received the news that Jo had given birth to their second child, a daughter named Francine. What he didn't yet know was that seven months later, Francine had died. He also didn't know that Jo and Marie could no longer stand the loneliness back at home, and had set sail north on a ship called the *Windward.* Aboard the *Windward,* Jo made a startling discovery: an Inuit woman named Allakasingwah told Jo that she'd had a baby by Robert. This was perfectly normal by Inuit standards, but Jo must have been stunned. Still, she was a strong, determined woman. She managed to accept that her husband had been lonely, that he still loved her, and that Allakasingwah had meant nothing more than to be kind to him in the fashion of her people.

Meanwhile, the next batch of mail had finally reached Robert. He was horrified to hear of Francine's death, and to learn of the hardships that Jo was enduring. He traveled south to where the *Windward* had berthed, and was finally reunited with his wife and daughter on May 6, 1901.

Three months later, Peary received another tragic letter. This one told him that his mother was dead. He was overwhelmed with grief, but he refused to leave the Arctic. In 1902, the *Windward* sailed south again, without Peary. He was overwhelmed again, this time by quiet sadness. He writes, "The loss of mother keeps coming to me. . . . Ah, Jo and Marie, was I criminally foolish in staying? Shall I really never see you again?"[2]

The expedition was a failure. Between an outbreak of what might have been the disease dysentery in the Inuit camp and terrible weather, Peary was forced to give up and return to the United States.

For a year, life seemed to return to normal. Peary went back into naval duty, going on missions to England and France.

In 1901, William McKinley died in office, and Theodore Roosevelt became president of the United States. Roosevelt liked the outdoors, and he liked explorers. He encouraged Peary to try for the North Pole again.

Marie Peary wasn't happy. She begged her father to stay home, saying that she didn't want people to think she was an orphan. But by this time, Robert had become obsessed by what he called the lure of the North. He *would* reach the North Pole.

Meanwhile, Henson became a porter for the Pennsylvania Railroad. He took the job so that he could see the United States. He also met and fell in love with Lucy Ross, a bank clerk in New York. The two decided to marry after Henson's next trip to the Arctic.

Peary and Henson set out again in 1905, on a ship of Peary's own design. It was named the *Roosevelt* in honor of the president.

The trip was overcome with problems. The *Roosevelt*'s engines partially failed. The Inuit guides were so reluctant to go on that Peary had to show them pictures of his wife and daughter, assuring them that he, too, was sorry to leave his family. The weather was so fierce that dogs were lost and men nearly starved. As one of the Inuit put it, "The Devil is asleep or having trouble with his wife, or we should never have come back."[3]

However, this may have been the trip when Henson, too, fathered a child with an Inuit woman. By the fall of 1905, Akatingwah had borne Henson's son, Anaukaq.

Forced to return without success, Peary began to plan a new trip. This time, every detail, down to the smallest possible variations in weather, was worked out in advance. Early in May 1908, he made the official announcement: His next expedition was, indeed, going to reach the North Pole. He said that he would use the "Smith Sound or 'American' route," which was a permanent stretch of open water discovered by American explorers. That would allow him a winter base one hundred miles closer to the North Pole than any he'd made before. He would use sleds, Inuit helpers, and Inuit dogs.

The refitted *Roosevelt* sailed north again on July 6, 1908. This time, the company reached base camp on Ellesmere Island without too much trouble, then prepared for the long winter to come. The temperature stayed about −50°F, and the wind carried tiny bits of ice that could pierce human skin.

By the end of February, the long dark winter was over and the sun had returned. Unfortunately, so had the thick Arctic fog. For six more frustrating days, Peary couldn't go on.

On the sixth day, March 1, 1909, Peary knew that he could no longer afford to wait. His plans depended on their keeping to a strict schedule. He and Henson, the other explorers, the Inuit helpers, and the dogs with their loaded sleds set out. Along the way, they built igloos, stocking each with supplies for the journey back. At different stages, part of the support team would return. By the last stage, only Peary, Henson, and four Inuit—Oatah, Egingwah, Seegloo, and Ookeah—remained. They had to struggle over breaking ice and through deep drifts of snow. But they kept going. Every day, Peary wrote down how far they'd gotten.

On April 3, the six men crossed thin ice over a lead in the Arctic Ocean. As Henson drove across, the runners of his sledge broke through. Henson plunged into the icy water. The quick-thinking Oatah grabbed Henson's hood and hauled him out.

It was almost a letdown when they actually reached the North Pole. Peary, for one, was so exhausted by the long, endless march north that he collapsed into a deep, exhausted sleep.

When Henson woke him four hours later and Peary realized where he was, pure joy swept over him. He wrote, "The Pole at last!!! The prize of three centuries, my dream and ambition for twenty-three years. *Mine* at last."[4]

Since the North Pole isn't an actual structure, it was difficult to be sure when they were exactly there. Careful measurements showed that Peary and his party were within three miles of it. Just to be sure, Peary took a dogsled and rode back and forth until he'd covered the area. Somewhere in that ride, Robert Peary became the first man ever to reach the North Pole.

Later, Peary wrote about what it meant to be at Earth's north pole: "East, west, and north had disappeared for us. Only one direction remained, and that was south. Every breeze . . . must be a south wind."[5]

Strangely, though, Peary's attitude toward Henson cooled. He barely spoke to him on the return trip.

Back in New York, the members of the Arctic Club of America were waiting with a great deal of nervousness. What had happened to Robert Peary? Would they ever learn his fate?

Then a brief message reached them from Indian Harbor, Labrador, Canada. It read simply, "Stars and Stripes Nailed to the North Pole." It was signed, "Peary." Everyone wondered if it was real or a hoax. Then a second message came in. It said, "Pole Reached. 'Roosevelt' Safe." This one, too, was signed "Peary."

That was it as far as Herbert L. Bridgeman, the club's secretary, was concerned. He announced, "Peary has reached the North Pole. He and I [had made up] a secret code." " 'Roosevelt' Safe" was Robert's way of saying, "Yes, I made it to the North Pole!"[6]

By April 23, Robert was well on his way back from the Arctic. Soon he was happily reunited with Jo and Marie. He wrote, "My life work is accomplished. . . . I have got the North Pole out of my system. . . . I have won the last great geographical prize. . . . I am content."[7]

The dogs that Robert Peary used in his expeditions are known as Inuit dogs—or Qimmiq (kee-meek), which is what the Inuit call them. They don't look like the Siberian huskies that are often seen in movies about sled dogs. The sturdy, powerful Qimmiq look as much like wolves as they do dogs. They have brown or gray fur and slanted brown eyes.

A Qimmiq

Unlike most dogs, they don't bark, but they do sometimes howl like wolves—which can frighten other types of dogs, and scare a great many humans, too!

It is believed that the ancestors of the Qimmiq lived in Asia about four thousand years ago. They crossed over into North America with the ancestors of the Inuit. Those people who kept going east finally reached Greenland and were stopped by the Atlantic Ocean. They settled there, and so did their Qimmiq. In fact, dogsled teams were the main way to get around on Greenland, since there weren't any roads and the Inuit didn't have boats. The Inuit of Greenland used dogsled teams until well into the 1960s.

The Qimmiq have a second job. They are good hunting dogs. They can track seals hiding under the ice by sniffing out the seals' breathing holes. When the Inuit caught a seal a Qimmiq had found, they would reward the dog with some of the meat. Qimmiq hunting packs could even help the Inuit catch polar bears.

By the late 20th century, snowmobiles were replacing sleds as the way to travel in Greenland. Working dogsled teams, as opposed to teams run for sport, were becoming rare. The Inuit and breeders in North America have been working to keep the Qimmiq breed alive.

Frederick Cook had accompanied Peary on an unsuccessful expedition to the pole.

Later, he claimed to have reached the North Pole before Robert Peary. His claim was finally proven false.

Controversy

On September 1, 1909, startling news arrived. Dr. Frederick Cook had once been part of Peary's expeditions—he was the one whom Peary had doused with water during a fire. Cook had gone off on his own, and now he claimed to have reached the North Pole on April 21, 1908, almost a year earlier than Peary.

After the first few expeditions to Greenland, Peary and Cook had quarreled. The fight was over a lecture tour that Cook wanted to make. He wanted to use information that belonged to Peary and Peary's expedition in a series of lectures for which he would be paid. Peary refused to give him the material for free. The two men parted ways, and feelings between them grew worse and worse over the years. By the time of Cook's announcement, the two men hated each other.

Peary was furious. On September 8, he sent an angry message to the newspapers. It said, "Cook's story shouldn't be taken too seriously. Two Inuit who accompanied him say he went no distance north." In a letter to the *New York Times*, he added flatly that Cook "has not been to the Pole on April 21, 1908, or at any other time."[1]

The media have always loved a good scandal. In Peary's day, there was no television, but every newspaper in the United States and much of Europe carried the story of the competing claims. They dubbed it the Polar Controversy. It was as important a story to the world of 1909 as the story of the first man on the moon in 1969.

Both Peary and Cook claimed that they were telling the truth. But there was some evidence against Cook. He was already being investigated for falsely claiming he had climbed Mount McKinley in Alaska. If he'd lied about that, had he lied about reaching the North Pole?

Cook seemed to enjoy being in the spotlight. Peary did not. He turned over all his evidence to General Thomas Hubbard of the Peary Arctic Club and fled to his home in Maine. His evidence was studied by a committee of representatives from many organizations, including national ones such as the U.S. Geological Survey and private ones such as the National Geographic Society.

On November 4, 1909, the committee made its decision and published it in *National Geographic*. They said the committee was "unanimously of the opinion that Commander Peary reached the North Pole on April 6, 1909."[2] That, at least, solved half the problem: Peary had not lied about reaching the North Pole. On December 15, he was awarded the National Geographic Society's gold medal. Several other medals followed from regional and Canadian geographic societies.

In Europe, people still wondered if Cook had been the first to reach the North Pole. When Peary received the English

Royal Geographical Society's medal in 1910, the medal said only, "For arctic exploration from 1886 to 1909."[3]

The Polar Controversy continued for years, even after the U.S. Congress declared Peary's story as true in 1911. When Cook was arrested on an unrelated charge of fraud, public opinion began to turn against him. Soon most people came to accept Robert E. Peary as the first to have reached the North Pole.

Meanwhile, Peary and Henson's friendship was strained. Reporters asked Peary why he had taken a black man to the pole instead of a white man. According to the *Pittsburgh Dispatch*, Peary had replied that by taking Henson, he would not have to share the glory of the achievement. He knew that the white establishment in the United States would dismiss Henson's contributions because he was black. For many years, that is exactly what happened. Henson was not honored by the white scientific societies. The African-American community, however, did acknowledge his accomplishments. The Colored Commercial Association of Chicago and the Boston Chamber of Commerce gave him awards in 1909. In New York City, a dinner in his honor was hosted on Madison Avenue.

Henson wrote a book about his adventures in the Arctic and with Peary's expeditions. Called *A Negro Explorer at the North Pole,* it was published in 1912. Although Peary was a little angry that Henson had used some of the expedition photographs without asking him, he secretly gave the publisher money to help advertise Henson's book. Peary also wrote a foreword to the book, in which he praised Henson's intelligence and determination.

Once Peary's lifelong dream had been achieved, he had to find something else to interest him. He soon became fascinated with the new science of aviation. He also saw political unrest stirring in Europe. Suspecting that a great war was coming, he began campaigning for the use of airplanes in the military. He lectured on the subject all across North America.

Peary lived long enough to see the start and end of World War I (1914–1918), and to see that he had been right about the use of airplanes both in the military and in peacetime. By 1918, he may have already been too ill to care about what was happening in the world. A blood disease called pernicious anemia was robbing him of vital red blood cells more swiftly than they could be replaced by medical transfusions. Henson came to see him, and the men relived some of their adventures. Perhaps the friendship was mended. Peary went into a coma on February 19, 1920, and died the next day.

He was not forgotten. In 1932, Marie Peary went to Greenland to oversee the building of a stone monument to him. The local people were doing the building. When Marie tried to pay them—not with money but in useful goods like guns and food—they refused. They told her, "You built this monument here because you love Peary, and we worked on it because we love Peary, and for a work of love, no one accepts pay."[4]

Matt Henson still received little notice, mostly because of his race. It was also difficult for him to find a job that would use his skills and intelligence. In 1913, President Howard Taft appointed him to a job at the New York Custom's House—as a messenger boy. He was promoted to clerk in 1927 and retired at age 70.

That same year, 1937, Henson was made an honorary member of the famed Explorers Club in New York. In 1946 he was honored by the U.S. Navy and the Chicago Geographic Society.

Forty-five years after Peary and Henson reached the North Pole, Henson and his wife, Lucy, were received at the White House. President Dwight D. Eisenhower held a ceremony commemorating Henson's contributions to the discovery of the North Pole.

Matt Henson died on March 9, 1955, and was buried in Woodlawn Cemetery in the Bronx. In 1987, after many petitions were filed, President Ronald Reagan granted permission for his body to be moved to Arlington National Cemetery. Henson was reinterred on April 6, 1988, next to the grave of Robert Peary. In 2000, the National Geographic Society posthumously awarded Matthew Henson its highest honor—the Hubbard Medal. Henson's great niece, Audrey Mebane, accepted the award at the Matthew Henson Earth Conservation Center in Washington, D.C.

As Henson once wrote: "Only man can get a vision and an inspiration that will lift him above the level of himself and send him forth against all opposition . . . to do and to dare and to accomplish wonderful and great things for the world and for humanity."[5] Robert Peary and Matthew Henson faced great odds in reaching the North Pole, but once they had their vision, they would not give up until they had accomplished this "wonderful and great thing."

FOR YOUR INFORMATION

An oil pipeline in the Arctic

In modern times, it seems almost impossible to understand the struggle that Peary had in reaching the North Pole. Modern jet planes like the big 747s regularly cross over the North Pole to get from the U.S. East Coast to Asia. But the region is still not completely explored or understood.

Besides humans, several types of animals make the Arctic their home. Birds such as the snowy owl and the bald eagle live there. Mammals include seals and walruses, both of which live in the icy waters; the caribou, or reindeer; the musk ox; the polar bear; and the arctic fox. Fish abound in the Arctic Ocean. Scientists have even found bacteria living on the incredibly cold undersides of icebergs.

However, all that wildlife may be in danger. Greenland in particular is being explored for oil and gas. Scientists have begun to find that modern pollution is turning up in the Arctic, even as far north as the pole. This pollution includes chemical waste, oil spills, and radioactivity. Tourism—allowing people to visit the Arctic—is a mixed issue. There is always a problem when people leave garbage and disturb the wildlife, but there is also the chance for ecotourism, tours that stress the ecology and educate people to protect the wilderness. There is also evidence that the Arctic ice may be melting. This may be part of a natural cycle, or it may be a sign of global warming, which some scientists believe is raising the world's overall temperature and seems to be the result of pollution.

Many colleges—including Peary's own Bowdoin College in Maine—now have Arctic study programs. Bowdoin houses the Peary-MacMillan Arctic Museum and Arctic Studies Center, named for Robert E. Peary and one of his assistants, Donald B. MacMillan, who also graduated from Bowdoin College.

Chronology

1856	Robert Edwin Peary is born on May 6 in Cresson, Pennsylvania.
1859	Charles Peary dies; Mary Peary moves with Robert to Maine.
1866	Matthew Alexander Henson is born on August 8 in Charles County, Maryland.
1868	Robert Peary attends boarding school.
1877	Peary graduates from Bowdoin College and becomes a surveyor; Henson runs away from home.
1879	Henson goes to sea as a cabin boy.
1881	Peary becomes a civil engineer for the U.S. Navy and is named a lieutenant.
1886	Peary takes his first trip to Greenland.
1887	Peary meets Henson, who is working in a clothing store; he hires Henson to accompany him on his second trip to Nicaragua.
1888	Robert and Josephine Diebitsch marry in August.
1891	Henson marries Eva Flint in April; two months later, Peary and Henson leave for Greenland.
1892	Peary and Eivind Astrup reach the northern coast of Greenland.
1893	Robert Peary, Josephine Peary, and Henson return to Greenland; Jo gives birth to Marie Ahnighito Peary; Jo publishes *My Arctic Journal*.
1897	Peary loses eight of his toes to frostbite; Eva files for divorce from Henson.
1898	Peary publishes *Northward Over the Great Ice*, begins three-year expedition to the North Pole.
1905	Peary and his crew attempt to reach the North Pole; they come within 200 miles of their goal.
1907	Peary publishes *Nearest the Pole;* Henson marries Lucy Jane Ross.
1909	Peary and Henson, along with four Inuit helpers, reach the North Pole on April 6; Frederick Cook claims to have reached the North Pole in April 1908, sparking the Polar Controversy.
1910	Peary publishes *The North Pole*.
1911	Congress declares that Peary, not Cook, was the first to reach the North Pole.
1912	Henson publishes *A Negro Explorer at the North Pole*.
1913	President Taft appoints Henson to the Civil Service at the New York Custom's House.
1917	Peary publishes *The Secrets of Polar Travel.*
1920	Robert Peary dies on February 20.
1927	Henson is promoted to clerk at New York Customs House.
1932	The Greenland monument to Robert E. Peary is built.
1937	Henson is made an honorary member of New York's prestigious Explorers Club. He retires from the Civil Service.
1955	Henson dies on March 9; he is buried in Woodlawn Cemetery in the Bronx, New York.
1988	Henson's grave is moved to Arlington National Cemetery, next to Peary's, on April 6.

Timeline in History

1587	English explorer John Davis sails up the coast of Greenland for about eight hundred miles.
1607	English explorer Henry Hudson, sailing for the Dutch, explores the North Atlantic.
1819	English explorer Sir William Parry sails halfway from Greenland to Bering Strait.
1829	English explorer John Ross discovers the precise location of magnetic north.
1845	Sir John Franklin sails for the North Pole and never returns.
1871	American Charles Hall sails for the North Pole; the expedition fails.
1888	Fridtjof Nansen makes an east-west crossing of Greenland.
1903	Orville and Wilbur Wright make the first manned airplane flight. Roald Amundsen successfully sails through the Northwest Passage.
1911	Roald Amundsen and four others reach the South Pole in December.
1914–1918	World War I is waged.
1926	Richard E. Byrd and Floyd Bennett fly to the North Pole and back.
1928	George Hubert Wilkins flies over Antarctica.
1937	Valeri Chkalov and Mikhail Gromov make a nonstop transpolar flight from Moscow to the United States.
1937	Russian scientists Ivan Papanin and his party are set down by plane on an ice floe near the North Pole to study the weather, ocean currents, and sea life.
1954	The Russian Arctic Institute discovers a mountain range below the surface of the frozen Arctic Ocean.
1958	The nuclear-powered U.S. submarine *Nautilus* crosses the North Pole beneath the Arctic ice cap.
1977	The nuclear-powered Soviet icebreaker *Arktika* becomes the first surface ship to break through the Arctic ice pack to reach the North Pole.
1986	Ann Bancroft becomes the first woman to travel to the North Pole on foot.
1992	Helen Thayer makes a solo trek to the North Pole.
2003	The first official North Pole Marathon is held.
2005	Led by British explorer Tom Avery, Barclays Capital Ultimate North Expedition re-creates Peary and Henson's trip to the North Pole, proving that it was possible for the men to accomplish what they claimed they had in 1909.

Chapter Notes

Chapter One
On the Edge of the World
1. From Peary's account, as related by his daughter, Marie Peary Stafford, in *Discoverer of the North Pole: The Story of Robert E. Peary* (New York: William Morrow and Company, 1959), pp. 68–74.

Chapter Two
Beginnings
1. William Herbert Hobbs, *Peary* (New York: The Macmillan Company, 1936), p. 8.
2. Ibid., p. 45.
3. Marie Peary Stafford, *Discoverer of the North Pole: The Story of Robert E. Peary* (New York: William Morrow and Company, 1959), p. 50.
4. Hobbs, p. 60.
5. *The Fate of Franklin,* http://www.ric.edu/rpotter/SJFranklin.html

Chapter Three
The Early Trips
1. Robert E. Peary, *Nearest the Pole* (New York: Doubleday, 1907), dedication page.
2. Marie Peary Stafford, *Discoverer of the North Pole: The Story of Robert E. Peary* (New York: William Morrow and Company, 1959), p. 95.
3. Robert E. Peary, *Secrets of Polar Travel* (New York: The Century Company, 1912), pp. 126–159.
4. William Herbert Hobbs, *Peary* (New York: The Macmillan Company, 1936), p. 91.
5. Robert E. Peary, *The North Pole* (New York: Frederick A. Stokes Company, 1910), p. 162.
6. Matthew A. Henson, *A Negro Explorer at the North Pole* (New York: Frederick A. Stokes Company, 1912), p. 42.

7. Josephine Peary, *My Arctic Journal* (London: Longmans, Green, 1893), pp. 227–228.

Chapter Four
The Pole
1. Robert E. Peary, *Northward Over the Great Ice* (London: Methuen and Company, 1898), vol. 2, pp. 97–100.
2. John E. Weems, *Peary: The Explorer and the Man* (Boston: Houghton Mifflin Company, 1987), pp.196–197.
3. William Herbert Hobbs, *Peary* (New York: The Macmillan Company, 1936), p. 365.
4. Weems, p. 270.
5. Robert E. Peary, *The North Pole* (New York: Frederick A. Stokes Company, 1910), p. 290.
6. Charles Morris, ed. *Finding the North Pole, by Cook and Peary,* W.E. Scull, 1909, pp. 48–49.
7. Donald MacMillian, *How Peary Reached the Pole: The Personal Story of His Assistant* (Boston: Houghton Mifflin, 1934), p. 289.

Chapter Five
The Polar Controversy
1. William Herbert Hobbs, *Peary* (New York: The Macmillan Company, 1936), p. 375.
2. *National Geographic,* Vol. 20, 1909, pp. 10008–9.
3. Hobbs, p. 401.
4. Marie Peary Stafford, *Discoverer of the North Pole: The Story of Robert E. Peary* (New York: William Morrow and Company, 1959), p. 215.
5. Reef, Catherine. *Black Explorers.* "Matthew Henson." New York: Facts on File, 1996, p. 63.

Further Reading

For Young Adults

Calvert, Patricia. *Robert E. Peary: To the Top of the World.* Tarrytown, New York: Benchmark Books, 2001.

Dwyer, Christopher. *Robert E. Peary and the Quest for the North Pole.* Langhorne, Pennsylvania: Chelsea House, 1992.

Ferris, Jeri. *Arctic Explorer: The Story of Matthew Henson.* Minneapolis: Carolrhoda Books, 1989.

Warrick, Karen Clemens. *The Race for the North Pole and Robert Peary in World History.* Berkeley Heights, New Jersey: Enslow Publishers, 2003.

Works Cited

Bryce, Robert M. *Cook and Peary: The Polar Controversy, Resolved.* Mechanicsburg, Pennsylvania: Stackpole Books, 1997.

Cook, Dr. Frederick. *My Attainment of the Pole.* New York: Polar Publishing Company, 1911.

Cookman, Scott. *Iceblink: The Tragic Fate of Sir John Franklin's Lost Polar Expedition.* New York: John Wiley & Sons, 2000.

Gilman, Michael. *Matthew Henson.* New York: Chelsea House, 1988.

Hayes, J. Gordon. *Robert Edwin Peary: A Record of his Explorations.* London: The Cayme Press Ltd., n.d.

Henson, Matthew A. *A Negro Explorer at the North Pole.* New York: Frederick A. Stokes Company, 1912.

Hobbs, William Herbert. *Peary.* New York: The Macmillan Company, 1936.

Hunt, William R. *To Stand at the Pole.* New York: Stein and Day, 1981.

MacMillan, Donald B. *How Peary Reached the Pole: The Personal Story of His Assistant.* Boston: Houghton Mifflin, 1934.

Morris, Charles, ed. *Finding the North Pole, by Cook and Peary.* no city: W.E. Scull, 1909.

National Geographic, Vol. 20, 1909, pp. 10008–9.

Peary, Josephine. *My Arctic Journal.* London: Longmans, Green, 1893.

Peary, Robert Edwin. *Nearest the Pole.* New York: Doubleday, 1907.

————. *The North Pole: Its Discovery in 1909 Under the Auspices of the Peary Arctic Club.* New York: Frederick A. Stokes Company, 1910.

————. *Northward Over the Great Ice,* two volumes. London: Methuen and Company, 1898.

————. *Secrets of Polar Travel.* New York: The Century Company, 1921.

Reef, Catherine. *Black Explorers.* "Matthew Henson." New York: Facts on File, 1996.

Stafford, Marie Peary. *Discoverer of the North Pole: The Story of Robert E. Peary.* New York: William Morrow and Company, 1959.

Weems, John Edward. *Peary: The Explorer and the Man.* Boston: Houghton Mifflin Company, 1987.

Wright, Theon. *The Big Nail: The Story of the Cook-Peary Feud.* New York: The John Day Company, 1970.

On the Internet

The Frederick A. Cook Society
http://www.cookpolar.org/index.htm

Matthew A. Henson
http://www.matthewhenson.com/

Peary and Henson Foundation
http://pearyhenson.org/

Glossary

Arctic
the far north around the world, above the Arctic Circle at approximately 66$^{1}/_{2}$° North.

civil engineer
a person trained to design, build, and maintain public works, such as bridges or roads.

crevasse (kruh-VAASS)
an extremely deep and often wide crack in the ice.

Eskimo (ES-kih-moe)
the old word for the Inuit; not a name they chose for themselves.

expedition (ek-speh-DIH-shun)
an organized journey, usually for exploration.

lead (LEED)
a narrow stretch of sea between the Arctic ice.

igloo
a temporary house made mostly of blocks of ice and snow.

Inuit (IN-yoo-it)
the native people of northern North America and Greenland.

ornithologist (or-nih-THAH-luh-jist)
a scientist who studies birds.

polar
relating to the North or South Pole.

scholarship (SKAH-lur-ship)
money awarded to a student to pay for college.

taxidermy (TAK-sih-der-mee)
the art of removing the innards of a dead animal and stuffing the hide so that the animal looks alive.

Index